D0854987

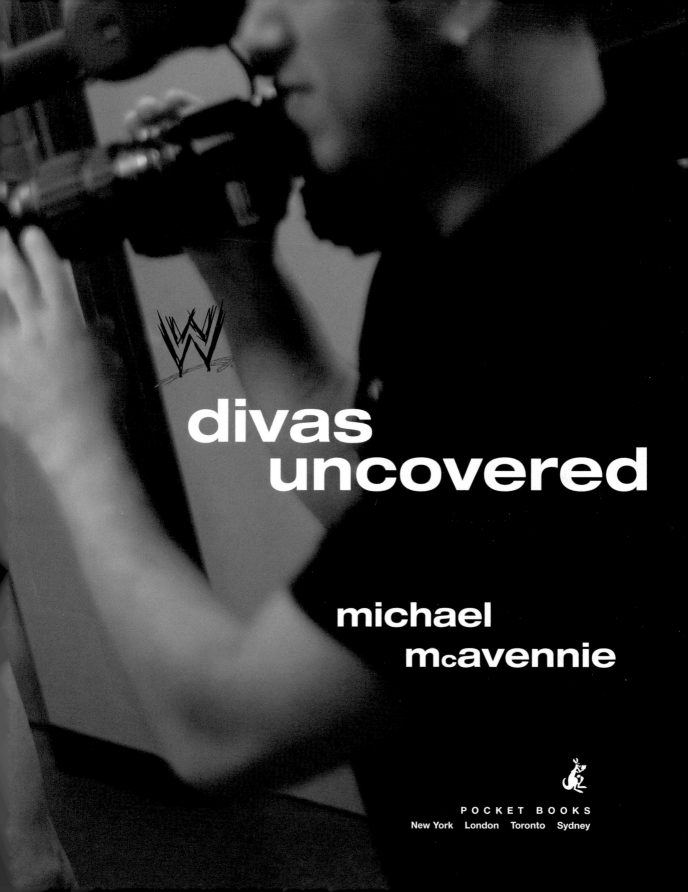

divas
uncovered

michael
mcavennie

POCKET BOOKS

New York   London   Toronto   Sydney

World
Wrestling
Entertainment®
B O O K S

POCKET BOOKS, a division of Simon & Schuster, Inc.
1230 Avenue of the Americas, New York, NY 10020

Copyright © 2005 by World Wrestling Entertainment, Inc. All Rights Reserved.

World Wrestling Entertainment, the names of all World Wrestling Entertainment televised
and live programming, talent names, images, likenesses, slogans and wrestling moves,
and all World Wrestling Entertainment logos and trademarks are the exclusive property
of World Wrestling Entertainment, Inc. Nothing in this book may be reproduced in any
manner without the express written consent of World Wrestling Entertainment, Inc.

This book is a publication of Pocket Books, a division of Simon & Schuster, Inc.,
under exclusive license from World Wrestling Entertainment, Inc.

All rights reserved, including the right to reproduce this book or portions thereof in
any form whatsoever. For information address Pocket Books, 1230 Avenue of the
Americas, New York, NY 10020

ISBN-13: 978-1-4165-1313-1
ISBN-10:   1-4165-1313-2

First Pocket Books hardcover edition October 2005

10   9   8   7   6   5   4   3   2

POCKET and colophon are registered trademarks of Simon & Schuster, Inc.

Designed by Richard Oriolo

Visit us on the World Wide Web
http://www.simonsays.com
http://www.wwe.com

Manufactured in the United States of America

For information regarding special discounts for bulk purchases, please contact
Simon & Schuster Special Sales at 1-800-456-6798 or business@simonandschuster.com

divas
uncovered

I prefer pinfall.
I like to leave
'em lying!

Trish

I need someone
who can keep up
and stay on the
same page
with me.

Stacy

I want a person to

look at my picture and

THINK they know what

I'm thinking,

but still leave a

little for them

to wonder about.

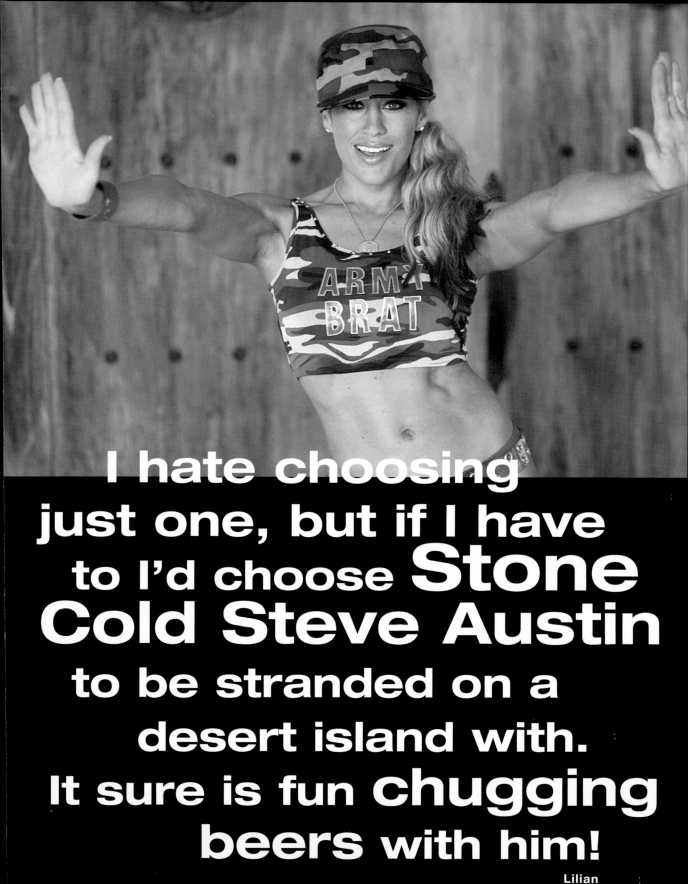

I hate choosing just one, but if I have to I'd choose **Stone Cold Steve Austin** to be stranded on a desert island with. It sure is fun **chugging beers** with him!

Lilian

Body language is very important and says a lot about a person, but I also think it's something that you can't put words to; you just kind of feel it.

Lita

I JUST *GO* WITH IT.

Maria

I think all DIVAS just love to have fun.

Lilian

One of my interests is motorcycle riding. I volunteer to give trophies to the pee-wees so I can watch the local Arena Cross races.

Victoria

I'm very spontaneous and wild. Dawn Marie

I see myself as an athlete who happens to clean up pretty good from time to time.

Jackie

I'm friendly,

confident, and

easygoing.

I love people,

and I love it

when they

come and say

hi to me.

Joy

You can always tell so much by a smile. I hope mine says that I am a warm, sincere person.

Michelle

I love taking my dog, **Chloe**, to a park in any city I travel to.

Torrie

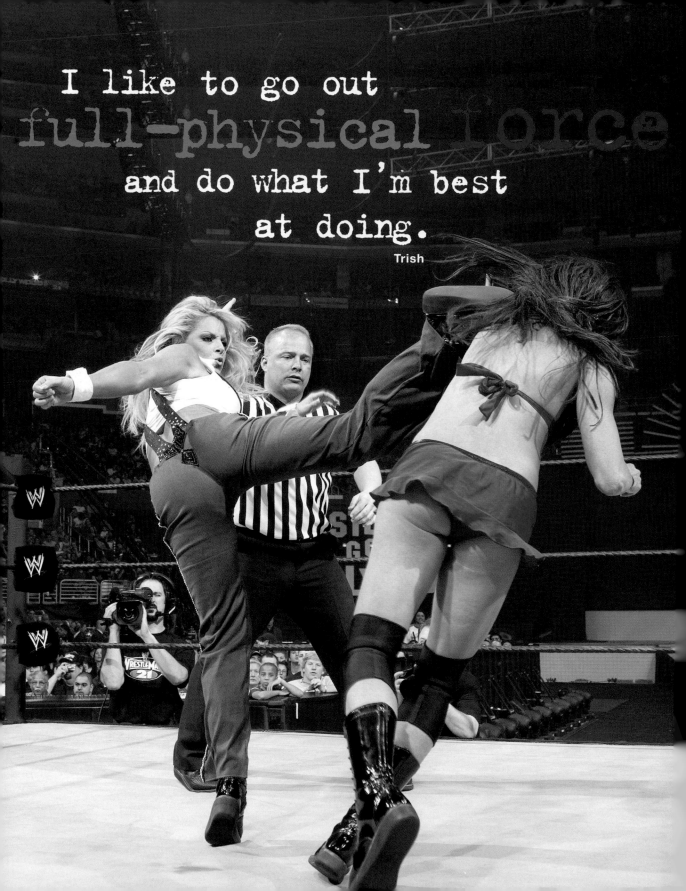

I like to go out **full-physical force** and do what I'm best at doing.

Trish

Ivory

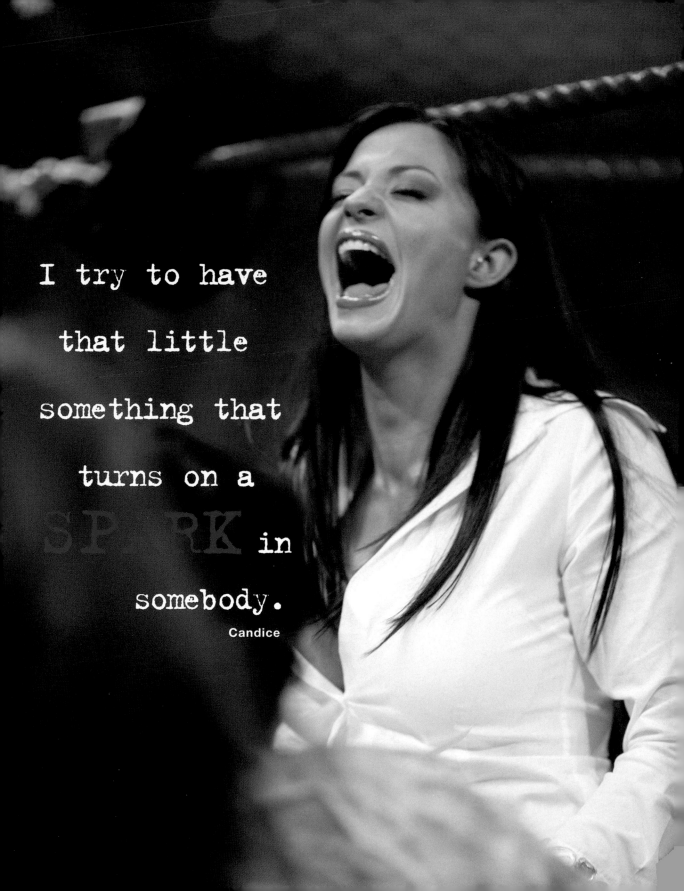

I try to have
that little
something that
turns on a
SPARK in
somebody.

Candice

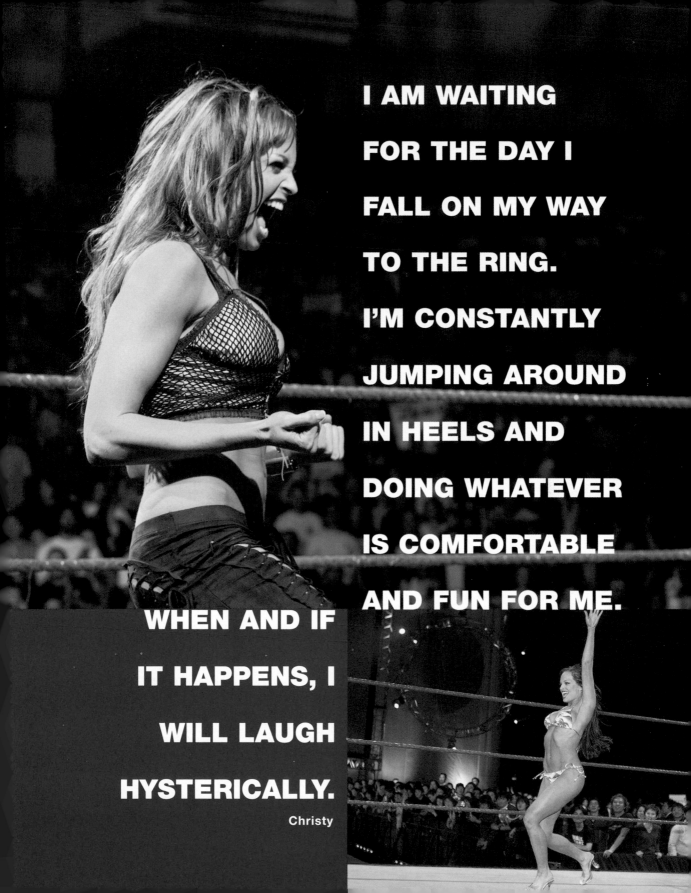

I AM WAITING FOR THE DAY I FALL ON MY WAY TO THE RING. I'M CONSTANTLY JUMPING AROUND IN HEELS AND DOING WHATEVER IS COMFORTABLE AND FUN FOR ME.

WHEN AND IF IT HAPPENS, I WILL LAUGH HYSTERICALLY.

Christy

I like being on any **beach**, where

I can feel the **sun** and **sand**, it

makes wearing a bikini

feel sexier.

Stacy

My fantasies are my fantasies.

Maria

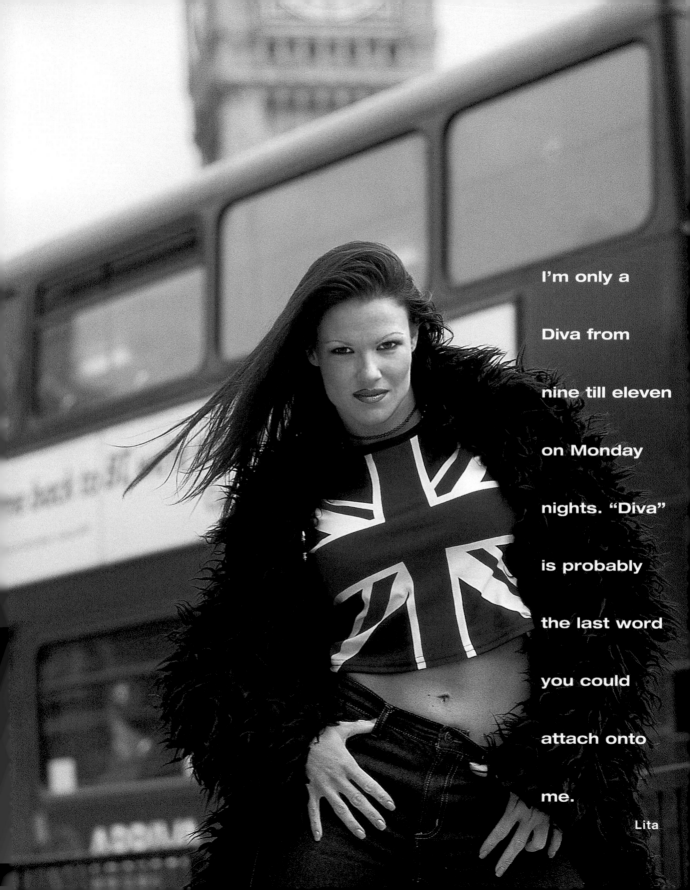

I'm only a Diva from nine till eleven on Monday nights. "Diva" is probably the last word you could attach onto me.

Lita

MY BODY LANGUAGE
SAYS I'VE GOT LEGS, AND I KNOW HOW TO USE THEM.

Stacy

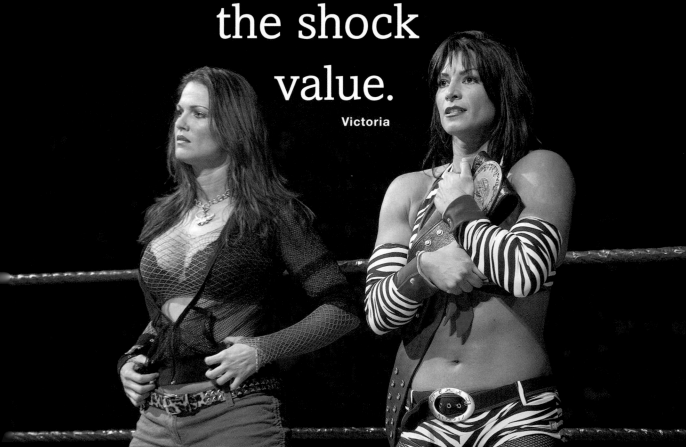

It's *exciting* for we Divas to get in the ring and do something new that will make the fans go, "I can't believe those girls *did* that!" We like the shock value.

Victoria

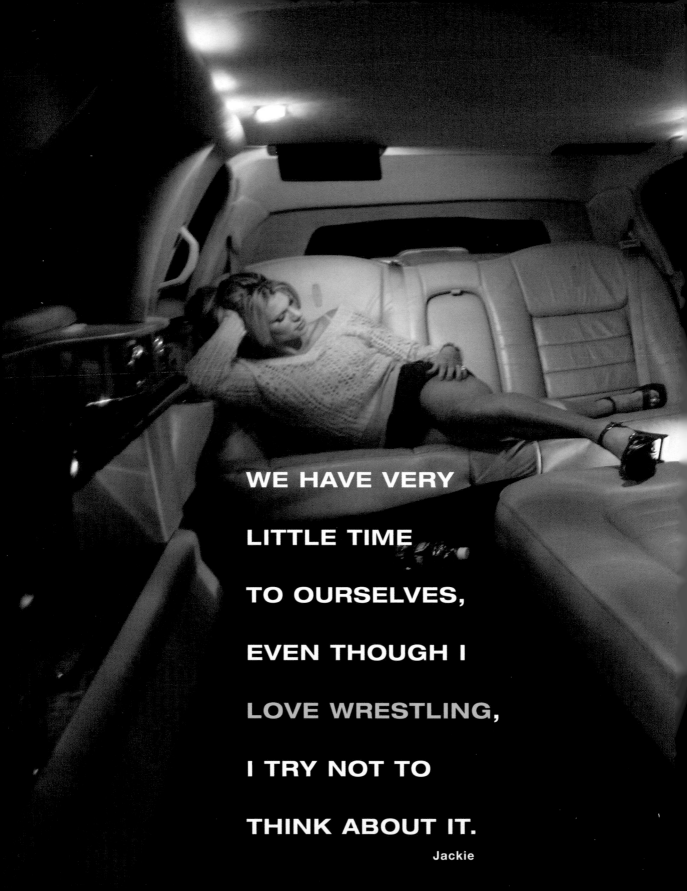

WE HAVE VERY

LITTLE TIME

TO OURSELVES,

EVEN THOUGH I

LOVE WRESTLING,

I TRY NOT TO

THINK ABOUT IT.

Jackie

Swimsuit
shoots…are tons of fun.

Jackie

People say my name suits me. There's always someone who has it far worse than you do, but if you look at how they persevere despite their disadvantages, it really puts things in perspective. What do I have to be unhappy about?

Joy

I ALWAYS DREAMED OF BEING WITH WWE AND NOW I'M HERE. I'M JUST **LIVING OUT MY DREAM.**

Michelle

IF THE FANS ARE
BEHIND ME, I FEEL LIKE
I CAN DO ANYTHING.

Torrie

I'M AN ALL-OR-NOTHING
PERSON; WHEN I DO OR
GO WITH SOMETHING, I'M
DEVOTED ONE HUNDRED
PERCENT AND WILL GIVE
MY ALL TOWARDS IT. I
NEVER GO HALFWAY.

Trish

You get the *sexiest pictures*
when you're wet.

Candice

I like to wear something that **stands out** and makes me **feel good.**

Christy

If I can count on a guy and he can make me laugh—and he better make me laugh—that's all I want. And I will give back tenfold.

Maria

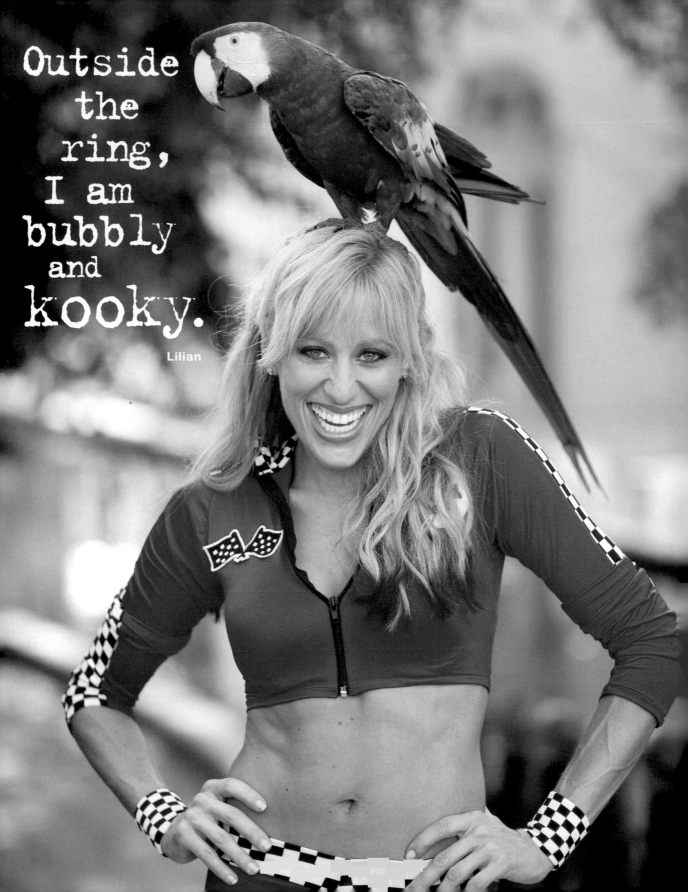

Outside
the
ring,
I am
bubbly
and
kooky.

Lilian

I'd want to be stranded on a deserted island with MNM's **Joey Mercury,** because of his insane charisma. Just ask him.

Lita

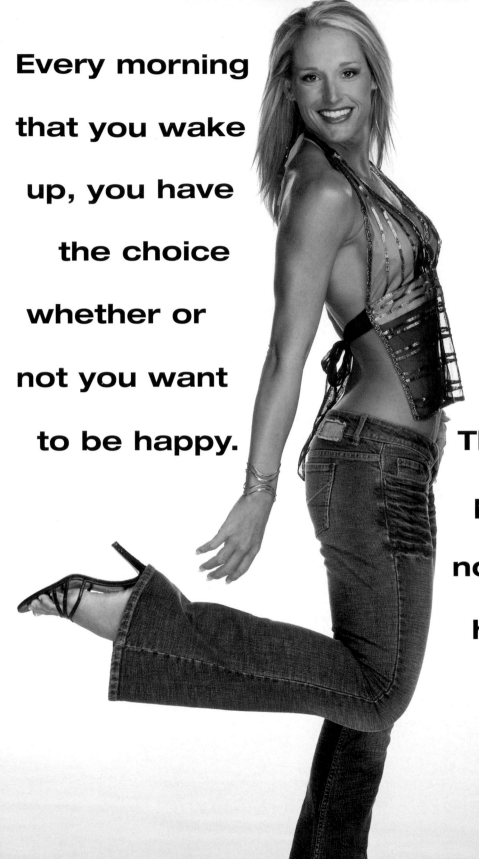

Every morning that you wake up, you have the choice whether or not you want to be happy.

There's no point in not being happy.

Michelle

My butt gets the most compliments from people.

Stacy

I TRY TO STICK TO A LOW-CARB, LOW-FAT DIET, BUT I WILL REWARD MYSELF.

Victoria

I don't wear

underwear. I guess

that *means I*

am  *carefree*

and *adventurous.*

Dawn Marie

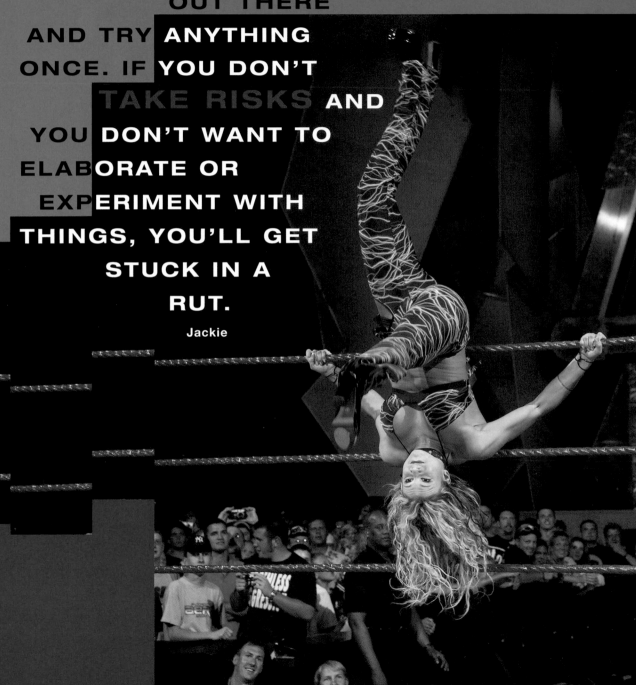

YOU HAVE TO GO
OUT THERE
AND TRY ANYTHING
ONCE. IF YOU DON'T
TAKE RISKS AND
YOU DON'T WANT TO
ELABORATE OR
EXPERIMENT WITH
THINGS, YOU'LL GET
STUCK IN A
RUT.

Jackie

Take me

anywhere

there's a

beach, and

I will love it.

Torrie

THIS **DIVA** LIKES HAVING DINNER COOKED FOR HER, TAKING A WALK ON THE BEACH, AND THEN ENJOYING A NICE, RELAXING DIP.

Michelle

You need to
follow your
heart more
than anything.

Torrie

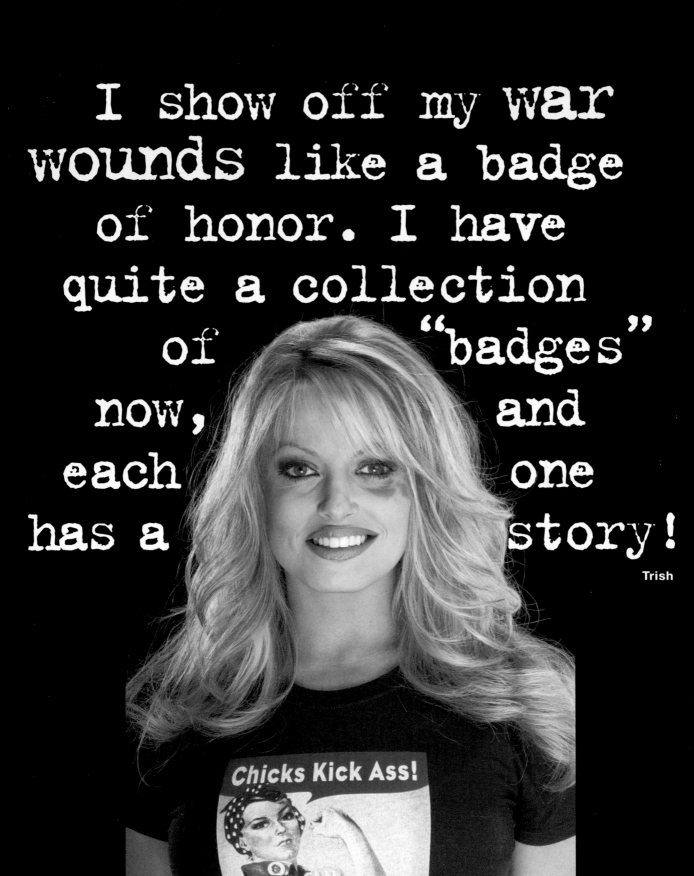

I show off my war wounds like a badge of honor. I have quite a collection of "badges" now, and each one has a story!

Trish

Chicks Kick Ass!

I DON'T REALLY FEAR WARDROBE MALFUNCTIONS, BUT IF ONE HAPPENS, I GUESS I'LL HAVE TO JUST GO WITH THE FLOW.

Candice

I know
who I am.

Candice

Do I like getting

wet? I was on

the swim team

for nine years, a

lifeguard for

about five

years, and a

swim team

coach for two

years. What do

you think?!

Lilian

YOU ALWAYS
DESIRE
SOMETHING
YOU CAN'T
NECESSARILY
HAVE.

Trish

PUSHUPS ARE A MAJOR PART OF MY WORKOUT, TO KEEP MY BREASTS PERKY.

I got a
brand-new
cell phone,
and I am
obsessed with
it . . . it's like, my
baby. My life is
in that phone.

Stacy

MY FANTASY IS TO WRESTLE IN A MAIN EVENT. IT WOULD BE A DREAM COME TRUE.

Victoria

I bring plenty of shoes with me wherever I go. Heels, **stilettos,** thigh-high **boots,** all the funky "stripper shoes" . . . forget it. I have *hundreds.*

Dawn Marie

I get nervous about performing ninety percent of the time. There's always that little self-doubt, but I don't let it get to me.

Torrie

I'm very high-energy... and a bit of a **drama queen.**

Victoria

One of my focuses is finding
ways to help expand my
charity ADORE, Amy Dumas
Operation Rescue & Education, at
www.adoreyourpets.org.

Lita

You can always feel the energy of the crowd.

Torrie

My Diva persona

is not really too

far removed from

my real persona.

Well, I guess I'm

not that bitchy!

Trish

other I have ever experienced. I

feel free and exhilarated.

Christy

I like my smile because I like

making other

people smile.

Christy

My favorite body part on myself is my **legs,** because man, I **love** to wear them **boots!**

Lilian

IF YOU HAVE A

BROKEN NAIL,

SMUDGED

MAKEUP, OR A

BAD HAIR DAY,

THEN MAYBE

THAT MEANS

YOU HAD

A PRETTY

GOOD

MORNING.

Lita

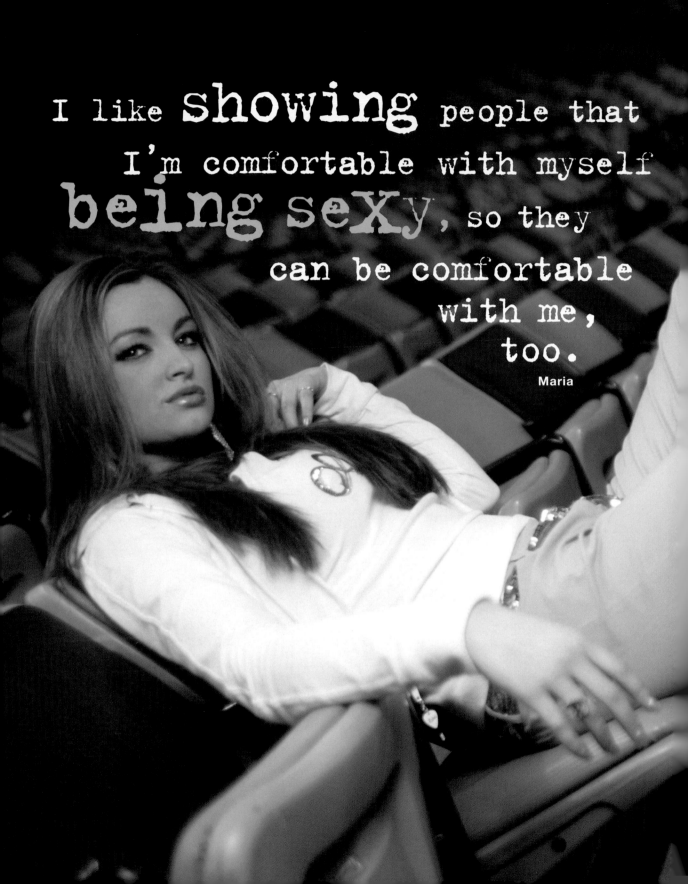

I like **showing** people that I'm comfortable with myself **being sexy,** so they can be comfortable with me, too.

Maria

DIVA

is just a name.

Stacy

My body language shows the passion I have for what I am doing.

Victoria

I like telling stories or setting a mood in my pictures. To just stand there and

take a picture is very boring. I want to make people look at my pictures.

Dawn Marie

Just ask anyone on the roster about my

"Tuesday runs"—an hour and a half each

and every Tuesday. I put on my Shox and

take off to explore every city we travel to.

Jackie

THERE'S A TIME TO GO OUT AND STRUT YOUR STUFF.

Joy

I don't think there's anything sexier than a woman who is comfortable in her own skin.

Michelle

My body language
conveys that I'm
not intimidated
by my opponent,
that I'm strong, and
that I'm going to
kick their
butt.

Torrie

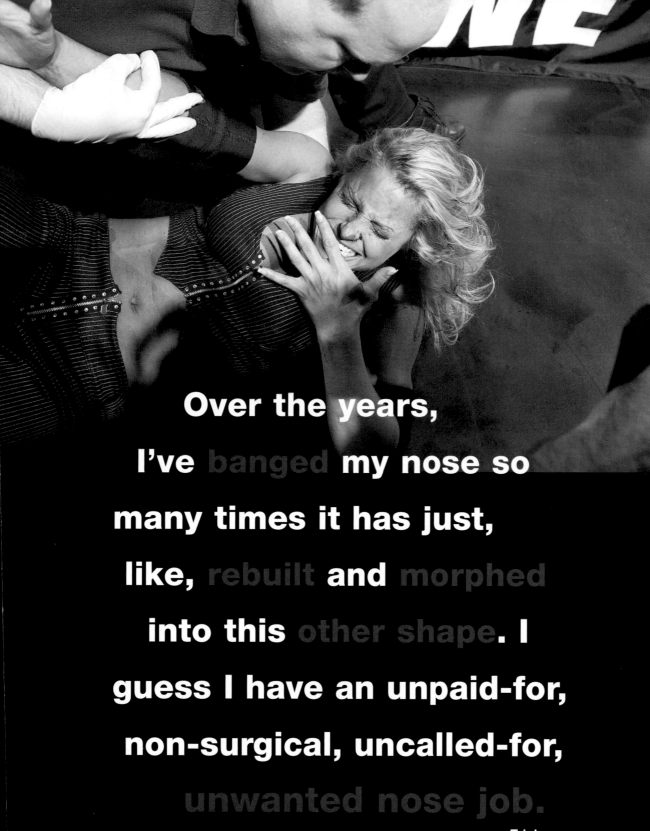

Over the years,

I've banged my nose so

many times it has just,

like, rebuilt and morphed

into this other shape. I

guess I have an unpaid-for,

non-surgical, uncalled-for,

unwanted nose job.

Trish

My motto is "*Work hard, play hard.*" I believe in always rewarding myself for goals accomplished.

Candice

IT'S IN MY HEMME BLOOD TO

THERE WAS NO OPTION WHEN I WAS

WORK HARD AND PLAY HARD.

BORN INTO THIS FAMILY OF HELLIONS.

Christy

I sang the National Anthem only two days after the attacks on September 11, 2001. That's a moment I will never forget.

Lilian

It was a great to go back to Mexico, where I started wrestling. Instead of a ten-dollar-a-night hotel, we were put up in a resort for a swimsuit shoot. It was all very, very full circle.

Lita

It's okay if
I'm always
considered a
babe.

Maria

A romantic evening . . . I would just want us to sit in, chill, and relax.

Stacy

I learned all my wrestling skills in the three WWE developmental territories. I'd like to think they are proud of the wrestler I've become.

Victoria

I TRIED TO NEVER LET MY NECK INJURY GET TO ME, BUT THERE WERE DAYS THAT I'D THINK, "I DON'T KNOW IF I CAN DO THIS ANYMORE." IT'S REALLY SCARY THINKING THAT WITH A SLIGHTLY DIFFERENT BREAK, I COULD HAVE DIED OR BEEN PARALYZED. YOU DEFINITELY LOSE YOUR INVINCIBILITY FACTOR AFTER SOMETHING LIKE THAT.

Lita

Being a WWE Diva means being appreciated for our beauty and strength, and having unique abilities.

I'M HAPPY, CONFIDENT,
AND CLASSY.

Michelle

It's exciting to know that anything could happen out in the ring.

Torrie

Hopefully, fans think of me as a perfect combination of both babe *and* athlete*. Maybe they can call me a* "babe-lete."

Trish

I travel with **Frankie,** my Ragdoll **cat.** I can't wait to get back to the hotel and **play** with him.

Ivory

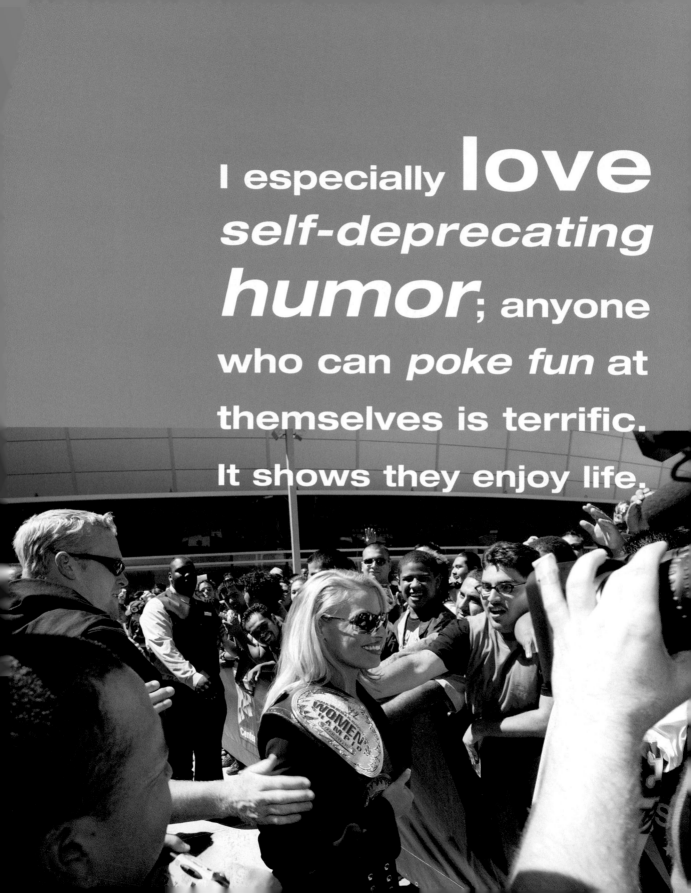

Nothing compares to ten thousand-plus fans screaming for you. It's quite a rush!

I like to win by submission...they're giving up and telling you that you're the more dominant **Diva** at that moment.

Lita

My photos are sexier than my normal personality. I like to talk with people, be nice and everything, but when I get in front of the camera, it's a complete release. I can totally go off.

Maria

I CAN DO ALMOST ANYTHING IN THEM.

I'M VERY COMFORTABLE IN HEELS.

Stacy

I don't know
if men are
intimidated
by me.
Ask them.

Jackie

I didn't think this is where I would be at this point in my life,

but now I don't know what I'd do without it.

Joy

Performing in front of a live audience makes me think, "This can't be work. I'm having too much fun!"

— Jackie

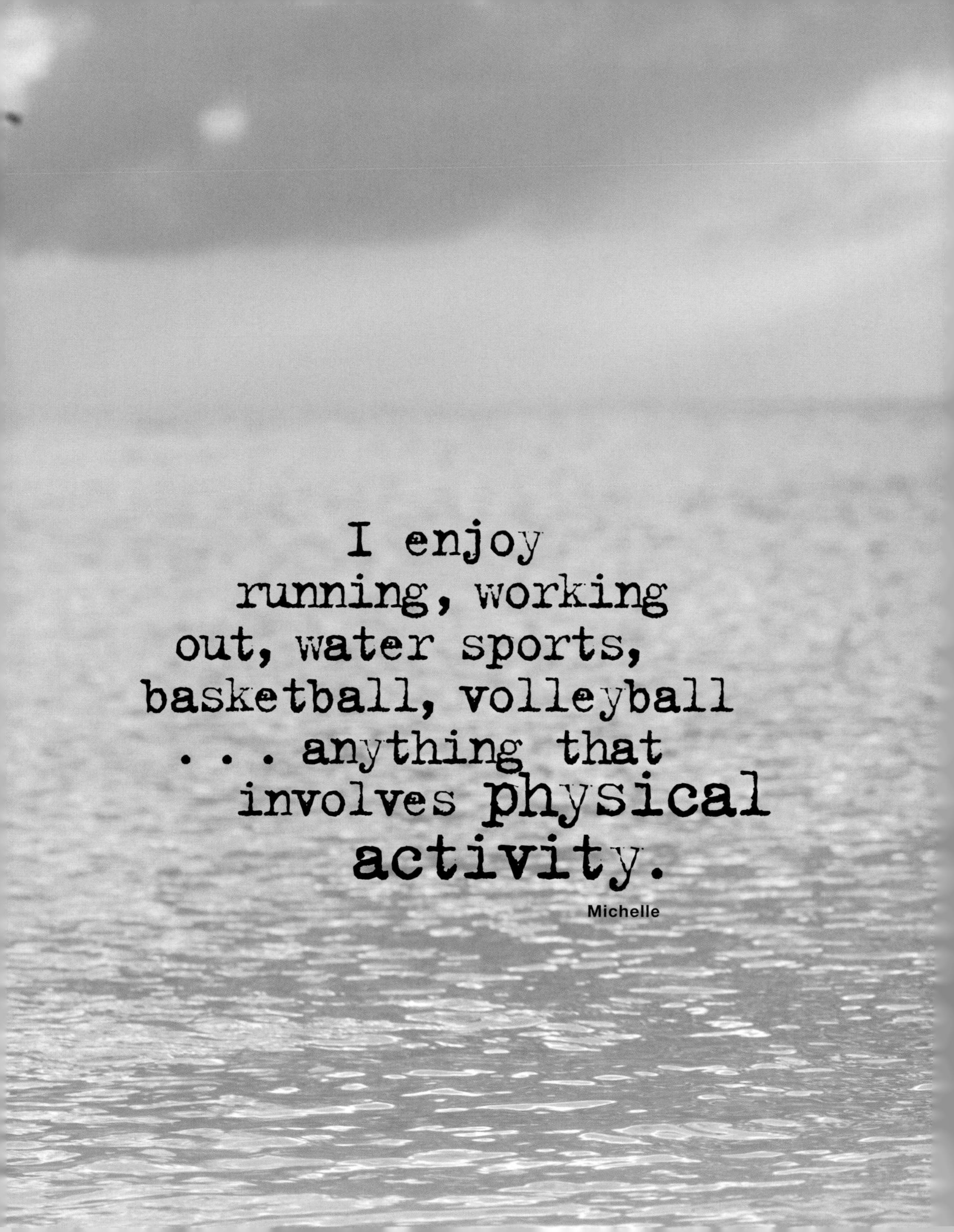

I enjoy
running, working
out, water sports,
basketball, volleyball
. . . anything that
involves physical
activity.

Michelle

Every performance is a new

crowd, a new town, and a

new dose of Stratusfaction.

TRISH

Trish

Hey, there's a time to show some ass, and a time to kick some!

Trish

BEING ENERGETIC IS JUST MY MAKEUP, IT'S MY CHEMISTRY. I WAS BORN WITH IT. I HAVE TO BE RESPONSIBLE ABOUT THAT AND EXPEND ENERGY SO I DON'T DRIVE MYSELF CRAZY.

Ivory

I actually get *shy* around a guy I'm interested in. But only in the beginning.

Christy

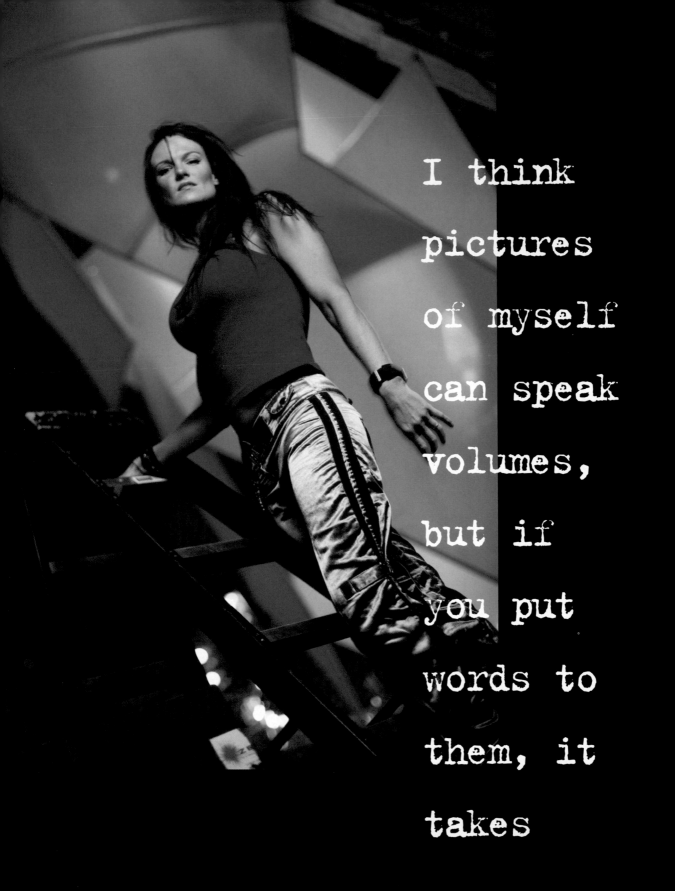

I think
pictures
of myself
can speak
volumes,
but if
you put
words to
them, it
takes

away the
magnitude
of how
much they
can say.

Lita

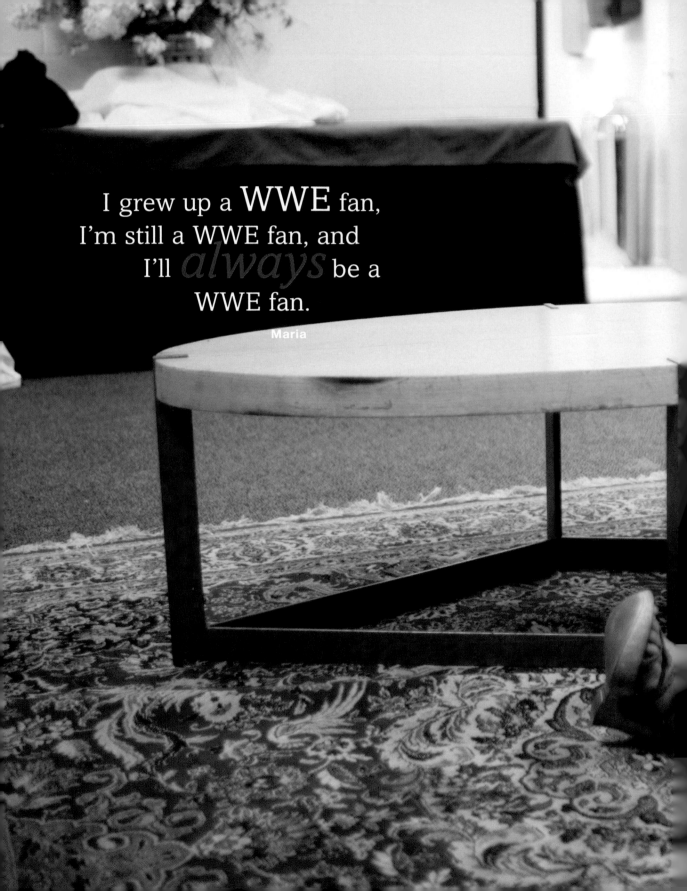

I grew up a WWE fan,
I'm still a WWE fan, and
I'll *always* be a
WWE fan.

Maria

If I'm going to get physical in the ring in my bra and panties, I'll pick something I know I'll feel comfortable in. Hopefully, it looks good too.

Stacy

It doesn't matter to me whether I *pin* someone or make them tap out. I just want to get the WIN

Victoria

I'm a fairly laid-back person who enjoys life. Not a lot bothers me.

Torrie

All shapes and sizes have the potential to make it in this, business. There's a flavor for every fan!

Trish

MY EYES ARE VERY TELLING. IF SOMEONE'S

CLOSE FRIENDS WITH ME, THEY CAN JUST

LOOK IN MY EYES AND

KNOW EXACTLY

WHAT'S GOING ON

IN MY LIFE AND

IN MY HEAD,

WHETHER I'M

TRYING TO MASK IT OR

NOT. I'M AN EASY READ.

Joy

*I'm just living
out my dream.*

Michelle

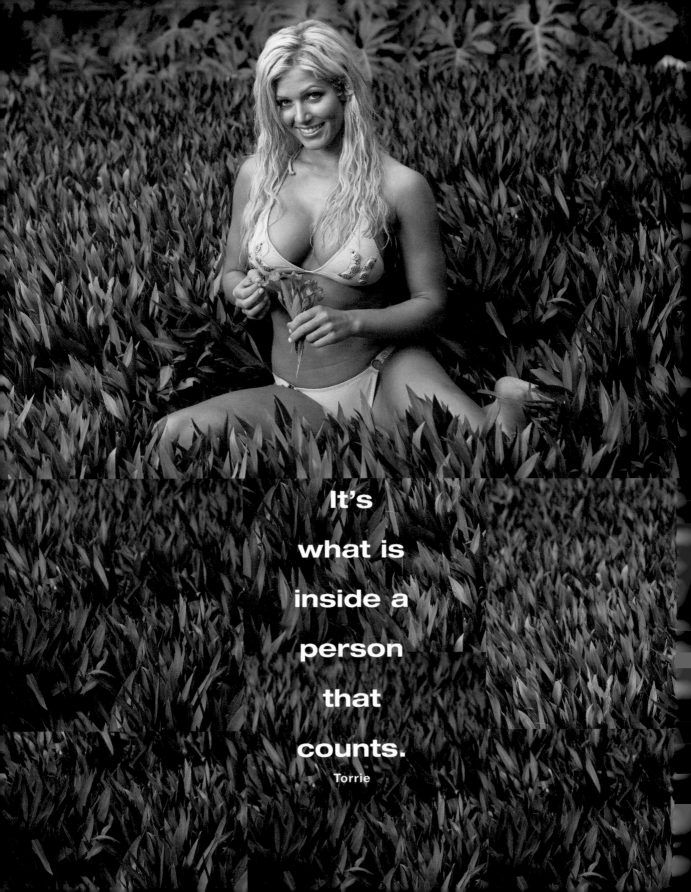

It's
what is
inside a
person
that
counts.

Torrie

BEING

HAPPY FOR

OTHER

PEOPLE

ULTIMATELY

MAKES YOU

HAPPY

INSIDE.

Candice

I THINK IT'S ALWAYS MORE EXCITING TO BE *SURPRISED.* I LOVE SURPRISES.

Christy

Some of us Divas

might be exhibitionists **at heart,**
but I don't think all of us are.

Stacy

It took us so long to re-educate the fans as to what we can do in the ring, but it has been a wonderful, exciting growth period, both for the fans and for us.

Trish

Being energetic is just my
makeup, it's my chemistry.
I was born with it. I have to
be responsible about that
and expend that energy so
I don't drive myself crazy.

Ivory

I have
energy and
enthusiasm for
everything
I do.

Christy

I like showing

people that I'm

comfortable with

myself.   Maria

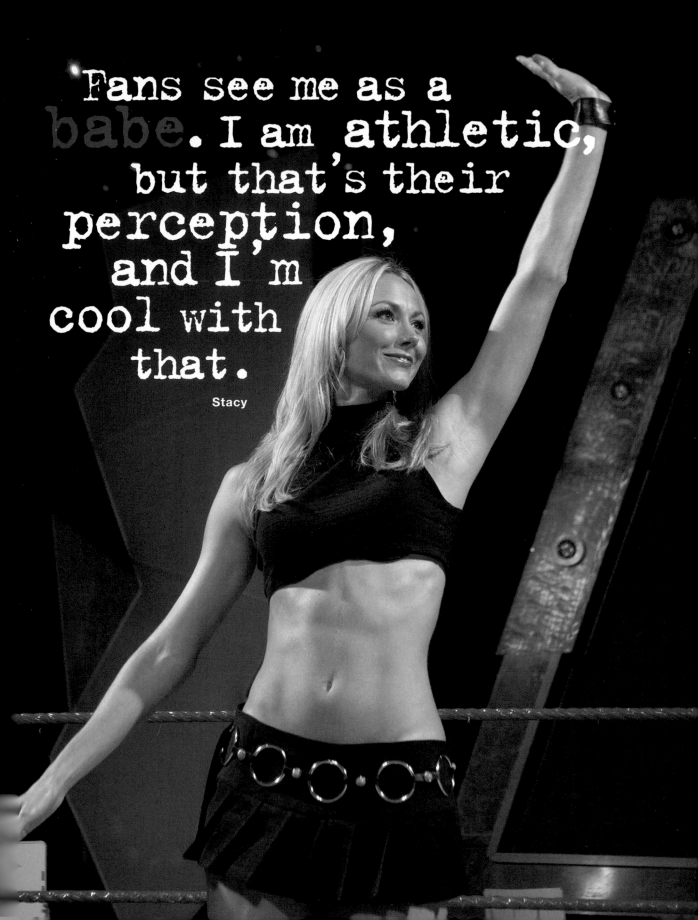

Fans see me as a babe. I am athletic, but that's their perception, and I'm cool with that.

Stacy

I'm carefree and fun. I love to laugh, and just say and do whatever I want.

Dawn Marie

I'm a
small-town
girl, and I
don't think
that'll ever
leave
me.
Michelle

I love comedy. I have a quirky side to my personality, and I love the chance to unleash it!

Trish

I have an
enormous
collection
of lingerie . . .

with no
man to show
it to!

Christy

We Divas love the attention, or else we wouldn't be here.

Victoria

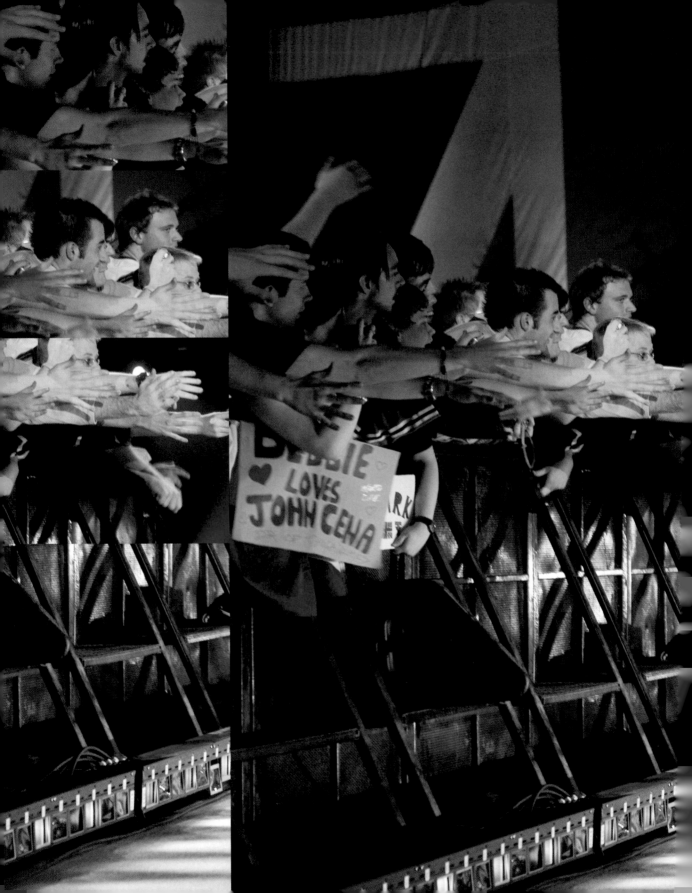

I always
want to wear
something
THE
FANS WILL
LIKE.

Torrie

Being **Happy** is

just my perception on life.

Stacy

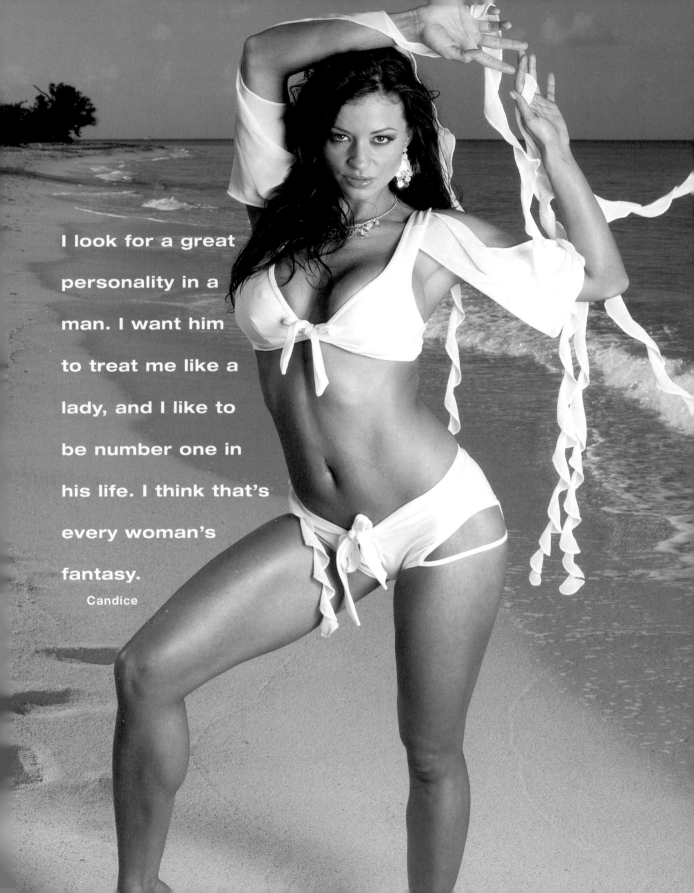

I look for a great personality in a man. I want him to treat me like a lady, and I like to be number one in his life. I think that's every woman's fantasy.

Candice

You're only as **good** as your last performance, period. And that's coming from the fans; it's the fans who keep you employed. So, when I'm behind that curtain, I know that if things *do* screw up, I have the tools and experience to fix it.

Dawn Marie

I can adapt to a lot of different situations, whether it's out there in the ring and doing something crazy, or being really presentable for the company at a corporate meeting.

Jackie

I love rooming with Christy Hemme. It's fun when you can share those **stupid moments** with somebody who will **appreciate** them, too.

Candice

I think WWE fans see me as a babe, but I KNOW that I have athletic ability.

Christy

I have a great job as a **WWE** ring announcer. If people are excited about meeting me, I make sure they know that **I'm excited** to meet them, too.

Lilian

My attitude is, "You are what you are, but you

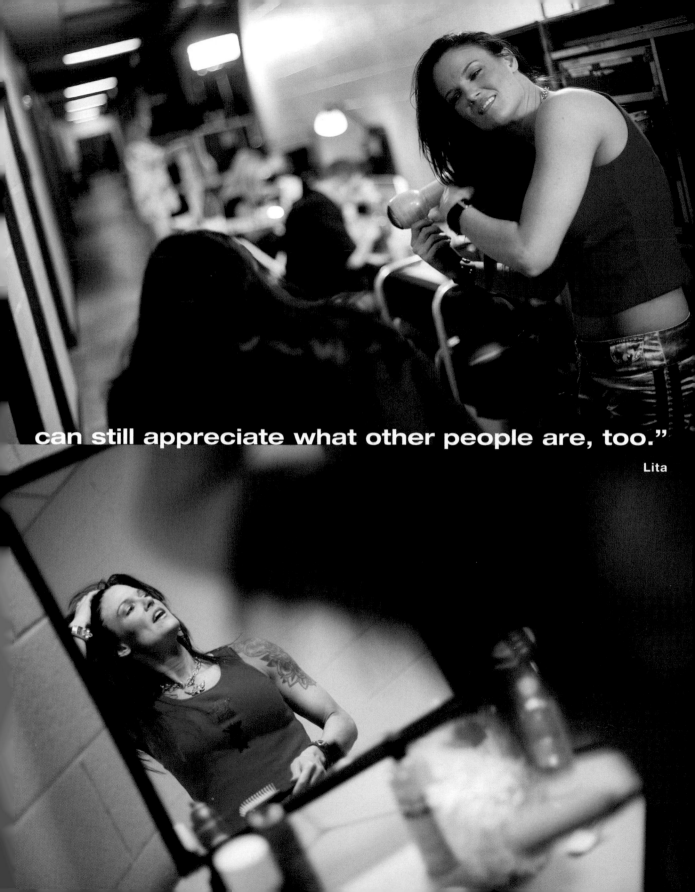

can still appreciate what other people are, too."

Lita

IF YOU'RE

CONFIDENT IN

YOURSELF, THAT'S

ALL YOU NEED.

Maria

I WORK HARD,

BUT I PLAY

HARDER. AND

THAT'S ALL I'M

GOING TO SAY.

Stacy

If you have passion for the business, it will show. If you *don't* have **passion for the business**, it will show. But if it's something you want to do, it can be a **tremendous experience.**

Victoria

I just want to excel here, reach the top, and learn as

much as I can from the people who have been here so

long and have such a wealth of knowledge.

Joy

I'm such a cutoff-sweats-and-sports-bra type of girl.

Michelle

Showing that you can be **sexy**, strong, and *independent* is the best thing about being a Diva. It's a great inspiration for other people.

Torrie

If a picture says a thousand words, my photos say "FUN times a thousand."

Trish

The thing that can launch you into **taking risks**, and feeling good and excited about it, is to be secure with the fact that if it was all gone tomorrow, you'd still have a pretty damn good life. You don't hang onto the fear of doing something risky.

Ivory

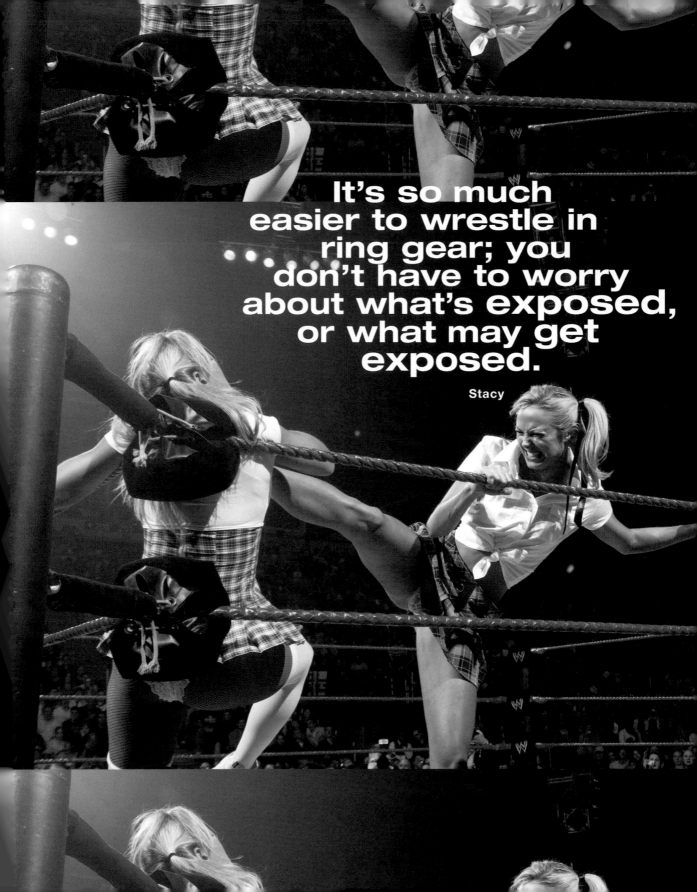

It's so much easier to wrestle in ring gear; you don't have to worry about what's exposed, or what may get exposed.

Stacy

I don't usually room with the

other **DIVAS.** There are certain

things I want to do that I can't

necessarily have another chick

IN THE ROOM WITH ME!

Maria

It's weird to think that anyone would be intimidated by me. Inadvertently, I guess I CAN be intimidating!

Lita

TRAVELING ON THE ROAD, IT'S IMPORTANT THAT YOU HANG OUT WITH SOMEONE YOU CAN GET ALONG AND BE WITH TWENTY-FOUR HOURS A DAY.

Stacy

ONE OF

THE BIGGEST

FANTASIES

FOR ANY

WOMAN IS

TO HAVE AN

"ON-CALL

MAN," A GUY

WHO WILL

COMPLETELY

CATER TO

YOU, NO

MATTER

WHAT, NO

MATTER

WHAT TIME

OF DAY.

Jackie

My photos say,
"Come get me."

Candice

I LOVE THE BEACH.

I'M HAPPY ANY TIME

WE END UP IN A

TROPICAL LOCATION.

Victoria

*My fantasies are simple—*cuddling, *eating cookies, and* laughing *at how goofy we are.*

Trish